P9-DGB-100

ANIMALS IN GROUPS

A Troop of
Chimpanzees
and Other Primate Groups

Richard Spilsbury

Heinemann
LIBRARY
Chicago, Illinois

www.capstonepub.com
Visit our website to find out
more information about
Heinemann-Raintree books.

To order:

☎ Phone 800-747-4992

💻 Visit www.capstonepub.com
   to browse our catalog and order online.

© 2013 Heinemann Library
an imprint of Capstone Global Library, LLC
Chicago, Illinois

Edited by Nancy Dickmann, Adam Miller,
   and Laura Knowles
Designed by Richard Parker
Original illustrations © Capstone Global Library
   Ltd 2013
Illustrations by Jeff Edwards
Picture research by Ruth Blair

Originated by Capstone Global Library Ltd
Printed and bound in China by CTPS

16 15 14 13 12
10 9 8 7 6 5 4 3 2 1

Library of Congress Cataloging-in-Publication Data
Spilsbury, Richard, 1963-
   A troop of chimpanzees, and other primate groups /
Richard Spilsbury.
      p. cm.—(Animals in groups)
   Includes bibliographical references and index.
   ISBN 978-1-4329-6485-6 (hb)—ISBN 978-1-4329-
6492-4 (pb) 1. Chimpanzees—Juvenile literature. 2.
Primates—Juvenile literature. I. Title.
   QL737.P96S646 2013
   599.885—dc23   2011038180

Acknowledgments
We would like to thank the following for permission
to reproduce photographs: Alamy pp. 26 (© Juniors
Bildarchiv), 29 (© Andrew Caballero Reynolds); Corbis
pp. 11 (© Karl Ammann), 16 (© Ocean), 41 (© Gallo
Images); Dreamstime.com pp. 4 (© Picstudio), 9,
24 (© Sergey Uryadnikov), 15 (© Sam D'cruz), 18
(© Aurell); iStockphoto p. 5 (© Gary Wales); Naturepl
 pp. 7 (© Miles Barton), 13, 27, 37 (© Miles Barton),
17 (© Karl Ammann), 19, 33 (© Florian Möllers), 20
(© Mike Wilkes), 31 (© Andy Rouse); Photolibrary
p. 40 (Robert J Ross/Peter Arnold Images); Shutterstock
pp. 8 (© PhotoSky 4t com), 12 (© JONG KIAM SOON),
23 (© Sharon Morris), 28 (© Galyna Andrushko),
32 (© Xavier MARCHANT), 35 (© FAUP), 39
(© Henk Bentlage)

Cover photograph of a happy family of chimps
reproduced with permission of Shutterstock (© Tiago
Jorge da Silva Estima).

Every effort has been made to contact copyright
holders of any material reproduced in this book. Any
omissions will be rectified in subsequent printings if
notice is given to the publisher.

Disclaimer
All the Internet addresses (URLs) given in this book
were valid at the time of going to press. However, due
to the dynamic nature of the Internet, some addresses
may have changed, or sites may have changed or
ceased to exist since publication. While the author
and publisher regret any inconvenience this may cause
readers, no responsibility for any such changes can be
accepted by either the author or the publisher.

Contents

DID YOU KNOW?

Discover amazing facts about chimpanzees.

HUMAN INTERACTION

Find out what happens when humans and chimpanzees come into contact with each other.

HABITAT IN DANGER

Learn how chimpanzees' habitats are under threat, and what is being done to protect them.

Some words are shown in bold, **like this**. You can find out what they mean by looking in the glossary.

Welcome to the Troop!

Chimpanzees are the **mammals** that are most similar to humans. Although they are the same basic shape as humans, adult chimpanzees are only the height of an average seven-year-old child. Their bodies are mostly covered in black hair. A chimp's expressive face has little hair, forward-facing eyes, and large ears.

Like humans, chimps are **primates**. Typical primate features include having five fingers and toes, with nails rather than claws. Chimps, humans, and gorillas are types of primates called **apes**. Apes have no visible tails. **Monkeys** (such as baboons) and a group including **lemurs** are the other types of primates. These primates usually have tails.

Chimps have long hands and fingers to grip objects. Although they usually walk on all fours, they can walk on two legs, just like humans.

Where chimps live

Chimps live in the wild only in central, west, and east Africa. They occupy a range of warm, damp **habitats**, ranging from the open spaces of tropical grasslands, called **savannahs**, to dense **rain forests**. Chimps usually live on and around trees, where they take shelter and find food. They are excellent climbers and use their strong arms to move and swing between branches.

A troop of chimps is sometimes called a cartload!

Troops

Individual chimps spend some of their time alone, investigating the world around them and searching for food. But chimps spend most of their lives alongside other chimps in groups called troops.

DID YOU KNOW?

The chimp's closest relative is the bonobo. Bonobos live in central African rain forests. They look like chimps but are smaller, slimmer, and hairier.

Who's Who in a Troop?

We can think of a troop as being like a school. In school, the whole school does not get together very often, and kids usually spend time in smaller classes. Similarly, much of the time, chimps from the same troop move around in smaller groups. The whole troop gets together when they find a source of food they can all eat, such as a tree full of fruit.

Within a troop

The small groups that form within a troop can be very different. An adult female may move around just with her **offspring**, with many other females and their young, or in a mixed sex and age group. Adult males may also form groups with other males. The bonds between all troop members are strong, but the bonds are especially strong between adult males.

Leaders

The leader of any troop is a male chimp. This is the **alpha** male. The alpha male gains his position by winning fights with other males, but also by making friends with various adults in the troop. He leads the troop when it finds food and when it meets or fights with other troops. The alpha male can usually **breed** with his choice of females in the troop. When the alpha male is not around, other males are more **dominant**, and older females are dominant over younger females.

DID YOU KNOW?

A troop of chimps usually contains around 40 individuals, but the largest troops contain over 100.

The alpha male in this troop is the second
adult from the left. There are adult females on
either side of him, one holding a newborn
baby. Other troop members include the two
young chimps on the right and adults in the
background of the photo.

Where troops live

A **territory** is an area that supplies animals with the **resources** they need. For chimps, the territory needs to supply enough shelter, water, and food for the whole troop. In a rain forest habitat, the troop members can find what they need in a fairly small territory. In open savannahs, their territory must be much larger, because resources are spread out.

HABITAT IN DANGER

Many African rain forests are being chopped down for timber, and savannahs are cleared for farms and settlements. This reduces chimp habitat and breaks up their territories.

When their habitat is destroyed, chimps may struggle to find the resources they need.

The alpha male **patrols** the territory edges, often in the company of several other males. Troop members learn from each other where the boundaries are and usually avoid going into another troop's territory, which might be right next to theirs.

Male troop members rely on each other to spot rival chimps, warn each other, and help fight them off.

Troop war

Sometimes males in one troop attack those in another. Troop wars may happen when there is not much food, or when males want to breed with females in another troop. The alpha male leads the troop to battle. The troop follows his lead in finding and attacking rival males. It is important for the males to stick together. If an individual is separated from his troop, he risks being injured or even killed by males from the other troop.

How Do Chimp Troops Communicate?

Communication is very important for chimps. Chimps can say how they are feeling or let the rest of the troop know where they are. Using sound is one of the most important ways chimpanzees can communicate. This is because troops often live in thick forests, where it is not always easy to see one another. Chimps make more than 30 different calls.

Personal call

Humans can recognize one another by their voices. Chimpanzees recognize one another using a **pant-hoot** call. This is a call that starts with soft "hoo" noises that get louder. These are followed by loud screams or barks, before returning to softer "hoos" again. Chimps pant-hoot when they are patrolling their territory, when answering other pant-hoots they hear in the distance, or when joining other members of the troop.

Different calls

Chimps use many different calls for different situations. Less important troop members use pant-grunt calls to show their respect to dominant chimps in the group. Chimps cough when annoyed and make a "huu" noise when puzzled. Young chimps whimper when nervous or when they cannot find their mother. This noise sounds like a repeated, high "aaah." When chimps find something unusual or dangerous, such as a snake, they communicate this to others using a loud "wraaaa" or bark call.

DID YOU KNOW?

Pant-hoots can be so loud that they may be heard around 1 mile (1.5 kilometers) away.

Every chimp's pant-hoot is different, and the pant-hoots in one troop are usually different from those in another troop.

Expressions

Like people, chimps use facial expressions to communicate their moods. However, their expressions do not mean the same things as ours. For example, a chimp grins when it is frightened, often after being disciplined by a dominant chimp. When a chimp sticks its lower lip out, then it is feeling calm and relaxed. A chimp stares long and hard or bares its sharp teeth to threaten another chimp.

Displays

Chimps also use body language and actions to show their feelings toward each other. Less important (**subordinate**) chimps moving toward a dominant chimp such as the alpha male will lower or bob their head. Sometimes they hold out their hand, too. To put them at ease, the alpha male might touch or hug the subordinate chimp.

This chimp is grinning to communicate that it is feeling uneasy, perhaps after being disciplined!

The most extreme chimp **displays** are when males become very excited. This is sometimes because of a heavy rainstorm, but more often because other males want to challenge their dominance. The male charges around and climbs trees. He breaks, drags, and throws any branches he finds. He makes as much noise as possible—for example, by screaming or banging his hands on large tree roots to make a drumming noise.

Excited male chimps may display by running around and making a lot of noise.

HUMAN INTERACTION

Chimps cannot speak, but some can communicate with people. A famous chimp named Washoe learned over 300 words in American Sign Language. She even taught her son how to do it!

What Do Chimp Troops Eat?

Chimps eat many types of food. They mostly eat fruits such as figs and coula nuts. They eat leaves, bark, and stems of plants, too. Chimps more rarely eat animals, ranging from caterpillars, ants, and eggs to monkeys and small deer. Their teeth are similar to human teeth, with sharp teeth for biting and tearing flesh or fruit, and flat teeth for grinding plant foods.

Finding food

A chimp troop usually starts looking for food at dawn and feeds mostly during daylight hours. On average, an adult chimp must spend about six to seven hours a day feeding to get the **nutrients** and energy it needs.

Chimps have very good memories for the locations of particular trees in their territories. They can remember where large fruit trees are, for example, and at what times of year the fruit is ripe. In one study, scientists found that chimps could locate a single tree in 12,000! Troops may travel many miles in a day to reach the best trees, rather than feed from trees with less fruit or unripe fruit.

HUMAN INTERACTION

Male chimps sometimes raid farmers' crops to steal papaya and pineapples, which are fruits that do not grow wild in the rain forest. They use the sweet fruit as gifts to encourage females to breed with them.

Chimps use their good
memories to locate ripe
fruit throughout the year
in dense rain forests.

Using tools

Chimps are one of a few types of animals that use a wide variety of tools. Here are some examples of how they use tools to reach or prepare foods and drinks.

- *Ants and termites:* These insects live in large **colonies** in nests and defend themselves by biting. Chimps poke sticks or grass into the nests rather than putting their sensitive hands inside. When enough ants or termites have crawled onto the stick, the chimpanzee sucks them off.

- *Honey:* Some chimps use a tool kit of different tools to get honey without being stung. They use a long club to break open nests of wild bees, narrow sticks to locate the honey inside, and strips of bark to dip into and spoon out honey they cannot reach.

- *Nuts:* Many nut shells are too tough for chimps to crack with their teeth. Chimps find a stone or short stick to use as a hammer. They collect nuts and place one on a rock or tree root. Then, they bash it with the hammer, eat the contents, and brush off the pieces of shell before breaking another.

Females tend to learn how to use tools more quickly than males do. This female is using a stick to eat ants.

Smashing open nuts with a rock requires patience and skill so that the food inside is not smashed, too.

DID YOU KNOW?

Chimps usually drink water from streams or ponds. When water is out of reach of their mouths—for example, when it is trapped inside a hollow tree—they make a sponge by chewing leaves. They hold the leaves, dip them in the water, and suck water from them.

Knowing what to eat

Chimps use their good eyesight and sense of smell to find food. They watch the feeding behavior of others in the troop to learn which foods are good or bad to eat. For example, chimps make high-pitched noises when they are eating food they like, but they make low grunts when they do not like it!

Chimps have a way of eating only the safe parts of harmful foods. Some fruits have tasty juice but poisonous seeds. Chimps wrap the fruit in leaves before chewing, to release the juice. They then throw away the leaves, with the seeds trapped inside.

Learning about safe eating is one of the benefits of living in a troop.

Some chimps look for particular bushes with leaves to eat that can stop them from feeling sick.

Medicine

Chimps, like humans, can become sick and die due to infections. Some chimps have learned to eat leaves from particular plants as medicine when they are feeling sick. They swallow the leaves whole. Inside the chimp's stomach, the leaves release an oil that is a powerful **antibiotic**.

DID YOU KNOW?

Chimps can learn how to get food by watching videos! Chimps in **captivity** were given two parts of a stick, and some tasty grapes were placed out of reach. Some chimps were shown a video of a trained chimp fitting the parts together into a long stick. The chimps shown the video quickly learned how to do so themselves. Those not shown the video took much longer to figure it out.

Hunting

Chimps are **predators** of animals such as red colobus monkeys, baboons, bush pigs, and small antelopes such as duikers. When food is plentiful, chimp troops will often feed on fruits and leaves as well as these animals. However, male chimp groups may choose to hunt these animals when food is scarce, especially during dry weather, when there is less plant food around.

Chimpanzees often hunt colobus monkeys, such as this one. Around half of a chimp troop's hunts are successful because of good teamwork.

Did You Know?

Chimps sometimes hunt small animals called bushbabies, which hide in holes in trees. The chimps use sharpened sticks as spears to jab into the bushbaby. Once injured, the bushbabies cannot run away, and the chimps break into the tree to catch them.

When hunting, chimps work together to corner the **prey** and kill it. For example, one chimp may wait in a tree to make a surprise attack on a monkey, while others move on the ground and up other trees to force the monkey toward him. The alpha male often shares the meat from the dead prey with the hunters and sometimes with females he wants to breed with.

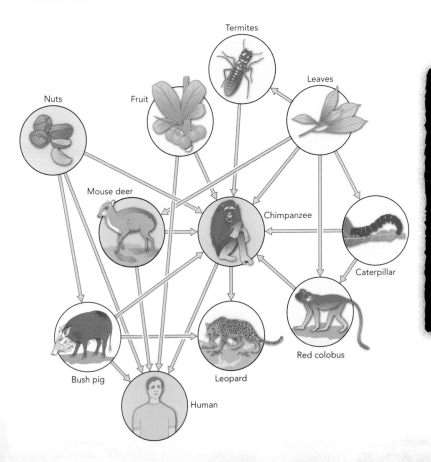

Chimps eat different living things in the rain forest—and are themselves eaten by other living things. In this rain forest food web, arrows point from each living thing to an animal that eats it.

HUMAN INTERACTION

Some people in Africa illegally trap or shoot chimps to eat as **bushmeat**. Bushmeat is a free source of meat for poor local people, but hunters also sell it to richer people from cities who like to eat this type of meat. Gorillas, elephants, and other wild animals are also killed for bushmeat.

How Do Chimps Care for Their Young?

Female chimps in a troop usually have one baby about every five years. The father shows little interest in his baby, but the mother cares for her young for many years. She relies on help from other troop members to look after the young until they are ready to be more independent.

Getting together

Female chimps can usually give birth for the first time when they are around 13 or 14. Males are often a little older before they can breed. This is because they have to become important enough in the troop for other males not to stop them. Males may display by waving branches to attract females. Chimps can breed all year round, and females are pregnant for eight months before giving birth to a single baby.

Newborn chimps

A newborn chimp weighs less than 3.3 pounds (1.5 kilograms). It is born with hair, including a white tuft on its backside, and it usually has lighter skin than its mother. The baby is too weak to stand or grip hard at first, so its mother holds the baby to her chest and belly hair for the first month. It **suckles**, or feeds, on her milk for about three minutes every hour.

HUMAN INTERACTION

When people kill adult chimps in a troop for bushmeat, they often capture the babies. They sell these young chimps as pets or even cage them to eat after they have grown.

A mother chimp carries her baby all the time until the baby is around six months old.

23

Independence

At about the age of six months, young chimps are strong enough to stand up and start to walk. They are soon able to climb in the branches of low trees. However, they remain very close to their mother. They ride on their mother's back when the troop moves and will never sit more than 16 feet (5 meters) from her. Babies start to eat solid food at around two years old, but they do not finish suckling until they are about five years old.

Young chimps slowly become more independent during their first two years of life.

Young chimps over the age of five spend much of the day in gangs. The gangs are usually all male or all female. They gradually roam farther and farther away from their mothers for short periods as they get to know their troop's territory.

Babysitting

A female chimp is so protective of its newborn baby for the first six months that it keeps other troop members away. Once the youngster becomes more independent, its mother may spend some time away **foraging**. The chimps, including older brothers and sisters, help one another with babysitting.

The toes on a human foot all bend downward, but a chimp's opposable big toe bends toward the other toes. This means they can grip, like human hands.

Chimpanzee foot

Human foot

Play and learning

Young chimpanzees in a troop spend a lot of time playing with other young chimps. Their games are very physical and involve wrestling, rolling, climbing, and balancing. They play games similar to human games, such as chase, tag, and king-of-the-hill, in which one tries to remain on a higher branch than the others. The young chimps also like to poke and tickle each other. While playing, chimps often put on a special "play face" expression with an open mouth and jutting chin. They pant fast, which sounds similar to a human laugh.

Young chimps develop great strength and agility. They move quickly through their forest habitats while playing.

DID YOU KNOW?

Young chimps sometimes carry around favorite sticks by day and sleep with them at night, like special toys.

As they grow up, chimps wrestle and fight for fun, but also to learn important life skills.

Playing is a lot of fun for the youngsters. However, it is also very important in helping young chimps learn skills that will be useful when they are adults. For example, moving fast on the ground and up trees will help them to escape from danger and hunt well. When they grapple and play-bite, they prepare for future fights. Playing with other males prepares young males for spending time with their own sex as adults, and to understand the importance of dominance in a troop.

HUMAN INTERACTION

In one part of Africa, young chimps have learned from older males in their troop how to break or damage traps that people leave to catch bushmeat.

Predators

Young chimps are especially at risk from leopards and occasionally from lions. Adults in the troop do their best to protect the young. If they spot predators, they warn one another with screams, ground thumping, and other displays. A chimp caught by one of these big cats is unlikely to survive, but some escape with bites and scratches. These are tended to by troop members, who remove dirt with their fingers and lick wounds clean.

Chimps under attack by leopards climb trees to reach safety, since they can climb faster than the cat.

Moving on

Youngsters become fully independent of their mother at around the age of nine or ten. Females then start to spend some time with other troops in nearby territories, and they eventually join one. Newcomers to the troop have low importance among other females, but males may want to breed with them. However, they do not have babies for several years, until they are accepted by other females who can support them in raising young.

Females in a chimp troop are often unrelated because some join from other troops.

Males stay in the same troop for life and do not move on. They spend lots of time in the company of males they have grown up with, sharing activities such as patrolling territory borders and hunting.

HABITAT IN DANGER

Logging and mining for valuable metals in rain forests in west Africa is not only endangering chimps and leopards through habitat loss. Building roads to remove logs and mined products also allows better access for hunters.

How Do Chimp Troops Relax?

The most common way a chimp troop relaxes is by **grooming**, often for hours on end. Grooming is removing soil, dried skin, insects, and other small things from hair. Chimps groom to keep their hair in good condition. This is important for keeping them warm at night and stopping the strong sunlight from burning their skin. They remove insects from their hair and skin, since these could suck their blood and affect their health.

How to groom

Chimps sometimes groom themselves, but they mostly groom each other. There are parts of their bodies they cannot easily reach. They hold back hair with their hands and use their delicate fingers, lips, and teeth to clean the hair. Chimps often eat some of the things they find in the hair.

Importance of grooming

Grooming is useful, but it is also a very important troop activity. It allows the troop members to bond. Sometimes a chimp offers part of its body or starts to scratch itself while sitting next to another chimp. This is an invitation to the other to groom.

DID YOU KNOW?

Some chimps crush insects they find while grooming between their fingers. Sometimes they crush them between leaves, so that their fingers do not get messy. Others place the insect on their arm and slap it to crush it!

This mother chimp is grooming her youngster.
Often, chimps will also groom those more
important than themselves in the troop.

Hanging out

Chimps often spend the hottest part of the day hanging out together in the shade. Females may rest and suckle their babies or watch their youngsters. Some adults sleep lying in trees. Often they bend branches into platforms called day nests that they can rest on.

Troop members take time out from the day's activities by hanging out in a cool, shady spot.

HUMAN INTERACTION

Sometimes tourists on **safari** come to watch chimps relaxing—but they need to keep their distance. One major reason is that chimps can catch some human diseases, such as the flu. They can sometimes die of these diseases.

Sleeping

At dusk each day, chimps make themselves a sleeping nest in leafy trees where they have been feeding during the day. They build their nests up to 100 feet (30 meters) high, to keep out of the easy reach of leopards. Sleeping nests take longer to build than day nests. Chimps choose a tree fork and bend or break large branches into a bowl shape across and around it. They hold them in place by weaving through smaller branches. Chimps then collect leafy branches to line the nest, so that it is comfortable.

Chimps sleep for around 10 hours each night in their own nest.

HABITAT IN DANGER

In Africa, millions of people are too poor to buy (or they have no access to) fuels such as gas to cook. Instead, many use charcoal, which is made by heating wood pieces. Much of this comes from trees growing in tropical forests where chimps live.

Do Other Primates Live in Groups?

Chimps are not the only primates that live in groups. Other primates form groups, for many of the same reasons that chimps do.

Gorillas

Gorillas are the largest primates in the world. Unlike chimps, gorillas have black skin on their face and have small ears. They eat mostly plant food, such as wild ginger, and occasionally insects, such as termites. Like chimps, gorillas have dark hair and live wild in Africa. There are two main types of gorillas. Lowland gorillas live in rain forests, while the hairier mountain gorillas live up in cold tropical mountains.

Gorillas live in groups called bands. These groups usually contain 5 to 10 members, but there can be as many as 30. The leader of any band is the biggest, strongest adult male. He is called a silverback. This is because older males develop gray, silvery hair on their backs. A band usually also contains several younger males, adult females, and youngsters.

The silverback decides where the band moves and sleeps and what it eats. He solves disagreements in a band, such as who grooms him, by using stares and grunts. He defends the band from any attacks by predators or other silverbacks that want to take over the band.

DID YOU KNOW?

Silverbacks roar, beat their chests, charge, and produce smelly sweat to frighten off other silverbacks.

This silverback gorilla is the leader of his band.

Baboons

Baboons are some of the largest monkeys in the world. They have a long snout similar to a dog's, small eyes, and long tails. Most types of baboon live in savannah habitats in Africa. They are more widespread than any other African primate and feed on a wide range of foods, ranging from crabs to grass.

Baboons live in large troops of between 10 and 200 individuals. Most baboons in a troop are females, their adult daughters, and the young of both sexes. There is a strict order of importance among these females that affects their offspring, too. For example, the young offspring of dominant females are dominant over adult subordinate females.

Males in a troop take a lead in looking out for danger and protecting the other baboons against predators such as lions or hyenas. Some males spend a lot of time with or near particular females they want to breed with. They carry, groom, and share food with her young and protect the youngsters from being hurt by dominant females.

HUMAN INTERACTION

Baboon troops raid farms to eat crops or even the young of farm animals, because these food sources are easy to obtain. They also move into towns and cities, where they steal food and cause damage to property. People may shoot or trap baboons to prevent the damage.

Baboon troops are unlike chimp troops because females remain in their mother's troop, but males join another troop when they are about five years old.

Ring-tailed lemurs

Lemurs are primates that live only in forests on the island of Madagascar and the Comoro Islands, off the coast of Africa. They are different from monkeys and apes in that they have moist, sensitive noses and they use their teeth rather than fingers to groom fur. The ring-tailed lemur has an unmistakable long, fluffy, black-and-white striped tail.

Ring-tailed lemurs live in groups called troops. Females are always dominant over males. For example, females decide on the trees and part of the territory where the troop feeds. Some male lemurs in a troop are also more dominant than others, but females rule the troop. Dominance in a troop is not fixed for a long time, as it is for chimps. For example, young females may challenge older females for dominance, and subordinate males may breed as much as the more dominant males.

Smelly communication

Unlike chimps, scent is important for communication among lemurs. Ring-tailed lemurs have scent **glands** in their wrists. These produce a smelly liquid that they rub on trees to mark their territory. The smell is a message to lemurs in other troops to keep away. In the breeding season, male lemurs compete using scent. They wipe scent on their tails and wave them around. The smelliest male is usually the most dominant!

HABITAT IN DANGER

Ring-tailed lemurs are under threat because people are clearing the dry forests they live in for farmland. Farmers often light fires to remove trees, but the fires can get out of control and burn large areas.

A typical lemur troop contains between six and thirty individuals.

How Can We Protect Chimps?

Chimps in a troop feed, hunt, travel, make nests, stay safe, and learn together. Being in a group means there are more eyes to spot dangers and opportunities. Like all animals that live in groups, chimps communicate in order to stick together and to divide up roles in the troop.

Chimps and people

Some people love to watch chimps, possibly because they are similar to humans. Tourists go on safaris to game reserves or national parks in some parts of Africa to see wild chimps. People also see chimps in zoos and wildlife parks. The best of these organizations work with scientists and charities to help wild chimps and **conserve** their habitats.

Tourists come to African countries to see chimps. This means that protecting wild chimps, rather than killing them, is a better way to earn money. Here a tourist is viewing chimps from a walkway suspended high in the rain forest.

HUMAN INTERACTION

In the Congo, one in twenty of the chimp population is killed each year for bushmeat. The bushmeat trade here and in other parts of Africa can only be reduced when people are educated about the reasons to conserve rain forest mammals—and are punished when they are caught hunting, buying, or selling wild animals.

Other people do not value chimps in the same ways. Some people see chimps as bushmeat, and they see the habitats they live in as opportunities for farmland or the sale of timber. Some keep chimps as pets, test drugs on them, or make them perform tricks in circuses. These are the main reasons why the survival of wild chimpanzees is under threat, and why it is important that the remaining chimps are protected from harm.

Wildlife rangers in Gabon check a truck used by forest workers for any hidden bushmeat. Patrols such as this help reduce the bushmeat trade.

Fact File

AGE AND SIZE

In the wild, a chimpanzee may live to be 50 years old, although some have lived longer in captivity. Although smaller in height than an average adult human male, big male chimps can weigh up to 170 pounds (80 kilograms). This is about a third of the largest gorilla's weight, two times that of a male baboon, and forty times heavier than a ring-tailed lemur!

HOW MANY?

There are around 200,000 wild chimps in Africa. Just a few decades ago, there were probably several million.

WHERE ARE THEY FOUND?

Chimps are found in 21 African countries. The largest populations are in Central Africa in the countries of Gabon, the Democratic Republic of Congo, and Cameroon. The smallest populations are in West African countries such as Nigeria, where chimps are at risk of dying out.

GETTING AROUND

Most primates usually walk on all fours. Chimps, like gorillas, are knuckle-walkers, which means they walk on the soles of their feet and knuckles of their hands. Baboons and ring-tailed lemurs use the palms of their hands.

CLOSE RELATIVE

Scientists have figured out that chimps have 98 percent of the same genes as humans. Genes are like instructions found in cells in living things for how something should grow, work, and develop. They estimate that chimps and humans had a shared ancestor (relative) from as recently as 5 million years ago. Since then, we have become different types of living things, but with many things in common.

This world map shows the area where chimpanzees live in the wild.

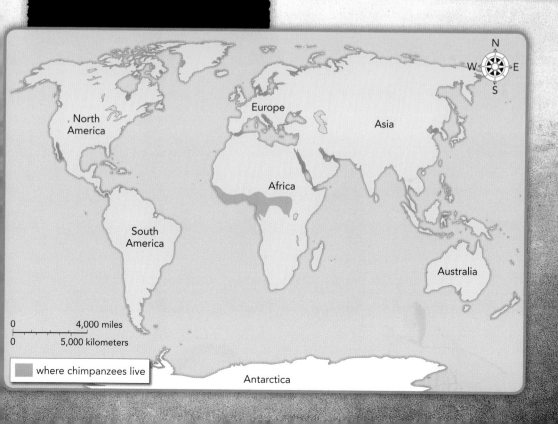

North America

Europe

Asia

Africa

South America

Australia

Antarctica

0   4,000 miles
0   5,000 kilometers

where chimpanzees live

Glossary

adapt change to suit the surroundings

alpha name for the leading male or female in a pack

antibiotic type of medicine that destroys or prevents the growth of bacteria and that cures infections

ape large primate that lacks a visible tail. Gorillas, chimpanzees, and orangutans are types of ape.

breed produce young

bushmeat meat from wild animals that people hunt for food

captivity being kept in an enclosed zoo or park, instead of running wild

colony group of animals that live together

conserve protect from harm or destruction

display show of actions to send a message to other animals

dominant more important; powerful

forage search for food

gland part of an animal's body that produces substances for the body to use, such as a strong scent to mark where the animal has been

grooming when an animal licks or cleans the hair and skin of another animal

habitat natural home or surroundings of a living thing

lemur type of primate with a long tail that lives wild in Madagascar

mammal hairy animal that feeds its young with milk from the mother's body

monkey type of primate such as a baboon with a dry nose, no whiskers, and long tail that climbs trees

nutrient substances in food that living things need in order to grow and live

offspring young of an animal or plant

opposable describes the way fingers can touch other fingers on the same hand

pant-hoot special loud call that all chimps make

patrol go around an area and check that it is safe

predator animal that hunts and eats other animals

prey animal that is hunted and eaten by another animal

primate animal belonging to the group of mammals including humans, apes, and monkeys

rain forest thick forest of tall trees that grows in hot, rainy regions

resource supply of something useful, such as food

safari trip to watch or hunt animals in their natural habitat, usually in Africa

savannah large, open plain mostly covered in grasses and shrubs, with patches of trees

subordinate less important

suckle feed a baby mammal on milk from its mother's body

territory area of land that an animal marks out and guards as its own

Find Out More

Books

Albee, Sarah. *Chimpanzees* (Amazing Animals).
    Pleasantville, N.Y.: Gareth Stevens, 2010.
McManus, Lori. *Gorillas* (Living in the Wild: Primates).
    Chicago: Heinemann Library, 2012.
Moore, Heidi. *Chimpanzees* (Living in the Wild:
    Primates). Chicago: Heinemann Library, 2012.
Throp, Claire. *Lemurs* (Living in the Wild: Primates).
    Chicago: Heinemann Library, 2012.

Web sites

www.discoverchimpanzees.org/become/start.php
See what it is like to be a chimpanzee by using this
web site. You can see how daily activities and choices
differ depending on whether a chimp is young,
female, or male.

kids.nationalgeographic.com/kids/animals/
    creaturefeature/chimpanzee
Visit this web site to watch videos and look at pictures
of chimpanzees.

wwf.panda.org/what_we_do/endangered_species/
    great_apes/chimpanzees
Find out about chimp conservation at the WWF
web site.

Places to visit

Would you like to see chimps for yourself? Although zoos and wildlife parks cannot give chimps the space they would have in the wild, many provide habitats to keep the chimpanzees interested and happy, with features such as climbing frames and trees and platforms at different levels to mimic the rain forest canopy. At this web site, there is a map showing the location of zoos with chimps in the United States. Use it to find the location closest to your home: **www.lpzoosites.org/chimp-ssp/locations.htm**.

More topics to research

At one time, people thought we were the only animals who could use tools. Today, we know that chimpanzees and many other animals use tools, too. Elephants use tree branches to swat flies, orangutans make whistles from folded leaves, and crows use twigs to pry insects from wood! Use the library and Internet to find out about other clever ways in which animals use tools.

Would you like to find out more about protecting chimps? You could read about projects such as this one run by the Jane Goodall Institute: **www. janegoodall.org/chimpanzees-protecting-home**.

Index